Written by Vincent Guillaume
Translated by Ciaran Traynor

Existentialism and Humanism

BY JEAN-PAUL SARTRE

BOOK ANALYSIS
Bright Summaries.com
BOOK ANALYSIS
Fifty Shades
of Grey Trilogy
BY E.L. JAMES

JEAN-PAUL SARTRE

FRENCH WRITER AND INTELLECTUAL

- **Born in Paris in 1905.**
- **Died in Paris in 1980.**
- **Notable works:**
  - *Nausea* (1938), novel
  - *No Exit* (1944), play
  - *The Words* (1964), autobiography

Jean-Paul Sartre was a French writer and philosopher. He was born in Paris in 1905 and died in 1980. Celebrated and at the same time rejected for his existentialist thinking, he is the author of several essays, such as *Being and Nothingness* (1943) and *Existentialism and Humanism* (1946). He also wrote several literary texts in which his philosophy and his definition of literature have a strong presence, including *Nausea,* a novel published *in 1938, The Flies, a play which first came out in 1943, and No Exit*, published in 1944.

In 1964, he turned down the Nobel Prize in Literature and published *The Words*, an autobiographical story about his youth. Also known as the partner of Simone de Beauvoir (French writer, 1908-1986), Sartre made a strong impression on his audience both with his writings and with his far-left political views.

EXISTENTIALISM AND HUMANISM

UNDERSTANDING SARTREAN EXISTENTIALISM

- **Genre**: philosophical essay
- **Reference edition**: Sartre, J.P. (1948) *Existentialism and Humanism*. Trans. Mairet, P. London: Meuthen & Co. Ltd.
- **1ˢᵗ edition**: 1946
- **Themes:** philosophy, liberty, responsibility, commitment, atheism

Existentialism and Humanism (1946, first published in English in 1948) is the retranscription, with some minor edits by Sartre, of a lecture he gave in 1945 at the Club Maintenant, which was set up after the Liberation of France. The lecture was extremely successful, which speaks volumes about Sartre's fame, although this fame was often accompanied by a poor comprehension of the philosopher himself. This is one of the reasons Sartre decided to make this speech.

In it, Sartre explains what his philosophy truly consists of, responds to criticisms which had been levelled against him, presents man in the full extent of his freedom and responsibilities, and proves that, far from being pessimistic, existentialism advocates action and commitment.

SUMMARY

EXISTENCE PRECEDES ESSENCE

Sartre lays out the main criticisms made of existentialism:

- Communists see it as a bourgeois philosophy of unrealistic actions;
- Catholics see it as a pessimistic philosophy which denies the importance of human efforts while also eliminating divine values.

Everyone accuses existentialism of disregarding human solidarity through a subjectivity which isolates the individual. Generally speaking, people find existentialism sad and ugly, even if the "wisdom of the people" (p. 24) seems just as depressing to Sartre.

According to atheistic existentialism, existence precedes essence. Before Sartre, philosophers had the idea that man is determined by human nature, like a manufactured object whose essence precedes its existence (its use, the production method and everything else which defines it comes before and determines its manufacture). But for Sartre, "man [...] surges up in the world – and defines himself afterwards" (p. 28): there is therefore no human nature, and man becomes what he makes of himself, or even what he wants himself to be.

Man is viewed as a project. He is responsible for himself, and existentialism wants to make him aware of this. This philosophy comes from a double subjectivity, both individual and personal. By choosing and acting individually with the intention of becoming what we want to be, we make of ourselves a project which is valuable for everyone, because what we consider the right choice for oneself reflects the image of man as we think he should be. Being aware of such responsibility for oneself and others, when man has to make a choice without knowing which values to hold on to, can cause anguish.

THE DEMAND OF CHOICE

Faced with the inexistence of God, man is left in a state of abandonment (an existentialist notion which goes hand in hand with anguish), and it is his task to draw his own conclusions: what is good is no longer written anywhere nor theoretically determinable. The choice is therefore given to man himself, who is "condemned to be free" (p. 34): he is entirely responsible for his passions as well as his interpretation of the world. Sartre gives the example of a student who is torn between two choices: staying by his mother's side or abandoning her to her despair and joining the Resistance in order to avenge his brother and help his country. When faced with such an impossible decision, man must choose between two types of morality:

- Immediate, individual help;
- Action on a larger scale, which is more ambiguous (who can predict if he will play an important role or an insignificant one?).

No fixed doctrine can resolve this dilemma. Choosing according to what feels right is also illusionary, since deciding that, in the end, you value your mother more than your country can only be proved by actually staying with her, and not merely by envisaging it. Similarly, in choosing someone to advise us, we have already decided which answer we want to hear.

In order to act, man must take into account the probabilities which directly concern his action and make it possible. Becoming a Marxist would imply counting on a well unified party and on comrades who will fight until the end, but that could very well end up not being the case because these other Marxists are also free. However, the probability of an international party being unified or not should not be taken into account, because it does not depend on the will of the person who is joining it.

Consequently, man must act without hope and without deluding himself, but must also not give up and do everything he can to succeed: existentialism is a moral code of commitment. Criticisms of quietism (favouring contemplation over action) are therefore unfounded: on the contrary, existentialism considers that man exists only through his action: without that, he is nothing. Trying to justify giving up on his dreams by thinking that he would have had the potential to realise them, if not for the circumstances, is not permitted. The characters of Sartre's novels appal readers because they are not just presented as cowardly or bad, but show that they are with their actions and their choices. "What people would prefer would be to be born either a coward or a hero" (p. 43): this determinist way of thinking is reassuring, because it implies that if you are a coward, you cannot do anything about it.

If there is no human nature, man does still have a certain universality (being in the world, being mortal, being free and so on) which is called his condition, and which defines him both objectively – since it is universal – and subjectively, since this universality is nothing if he cannot be defined in relation to it. And it is in this situation, which is to say in a specific sociohistorical context, that man is defined in relation to the universality of human condition. He does this in a multitude of individual projects, which are nonetheless never completely foreign to him because they are always based on the same universal human characteristics, including freedom (which allows man to define himself through his choices). Choosing is an absolute, an element of the human condition, and every subsequent action will be understandable anybody in any time period, without for all that losing its relativity as a result of the concrete situation in which it was made.

The criticism made of existentialism concerning its supposed subjectivism ("Then it does not matter what you do," p. 47) is baseless, because choice is an inevitable absolute: faced with a situation, choosing to not choose is not an option, but an illusion. On the other hand, although we have no scale of values to refer to, choice is neither a gratuitous action nor a whim, as it is done in the moment and involves the whole of humanity.

OTHERS, THE CONDITION OF OUR EXISTENCE

Existentialism makes Descartes' (French philosopher, mathematician and physicist, 1596-1650) cogito "I think, therefore I am" the only absolute truth: consciousness finds itself and can see that it exists by the very fact of thinking. However, in existentialism, we not only know ourselves through the cogito, but we also discover others: "we are just as certain of the other as we are of ourselves" (p. 45). Moreover, the other is the condition of our existence in the sense that we can only be defined (for example, as being mean, spiritual and so on) in relation to how others see us. In recognising the other as "a freedom which confronts mine, and cannot think without doing so either against or for me" (p. 45), we discover inter-subjectivity, a world where men define each other.

One of the criticisms levelled at existentialism is "You are unable to judge others" (p. 50). If man chooses his plan clearly and sincerely, there is indeed nothing to criticise. But we can judge that choices are based on truth and coherence, and others on bad faith, such as the refusal of freedom or hiding behind determinism. Furthermore, freedom is the ultimate meaning of acts of good faith, and this freedom as a goal (rather than as an element of the human condition) depends on freedom for all: in making your own freedom an objective, you cannot help but make the freedom of everyone an objective too. With regard to authenticity, we can therefore judge those who refuse this freedom. Sartre calls those who invent determinist excuses cowards, and those who claim that human existence was necessary (in other words, those who consider it a right and not chance, and therefore see their positions and privileges as definitive) scum.

A final criticism claims that "your values are not serious, since you choose them yourselves" (p. 54). Sartre responds that once you eliminate God, there is no other solution. Theoretically, life has no meaning: it is man who gives it meaning by living it. Human community is therefore possible, which brings Sartre to talk about two forms of humanism: the classic form, which he has criticised in his writings, glorifies humanity as an end and a higher value: existentialist humanism exempts man from judging himself, not considering him as a finished article because he is always a work in progress. It sees man as existing by trying to reach transcendent goals, by chasing not what he is but what he can become, all the while staying on a human plane of his own subjectivity. It is a humanism because man is considered the only maker of laws, finding fulfilment in searching for objectives that are beyond him.

CONTEXT

When Sartre gave his lecture *Existentialism and Humanism*, he was already very well known for literary works such as *Nausea* and the first two volumes of *The Roads to Freedom* (*The Age of Reason* and *The Reprieve, 1945, first published in English in 1947*), which he had just brought out. His literature, which offers a more accessible glimpse into his mind, is a parallel development of the philosophy which he had been developing since the 1930s and which culminated in *Being and Nothingness* (1943). This complex philosophical text helped to confirm Sartre's celebrity, at the cost of a poor understanding of his work.

People misjudged existentialism and linked it with ugliness and cynicism, similar to Sartre's literary characters, who are cowardly and frighteningly clear-sighted. The press used the most shocking parts of Sartre's writings completely out of context. Intellectuals, without even attempting to understand him, simply branded him inhumane and amoral and condemned his philosophy of freedom as a philosophy of despair:

- Marxists accused him of quietism and of a subjectivity which was incapable of seeing beyond itself to conceive the world.
- Catholics accused him of eliminating moral values which have been in place since the dawn of time, all in the name of freedom. They also believed he was challenging eve-

rything humanity had accomplished with his dangerous relativism.

Sartre was therefore a scandalous writer, even if opinion remained divided. His work did indeed find its supporters and was praised for its literary value. It was also enthusiastically received by a young audience, the very people Sartre was accused of trying to corrupt.

It therefore seems natural that Sartre would try to set the record straight by responding to his critics. In doing this, he justified his existentialism and guaranteed it a place in the intellectual landscape of the time. This was not his first step down that road either: he had already explained himself in the communist weekly newspaper *Action* in December 1944 and had just set up the journal *Les Temps Modernes* (*Modern Times*), the first issue of which came out in October 1945, in order to ensure that it followed his doctrine closely. Generally speaking, Sartre wanted to move towards the ideas of the left and fight for the community at the sides of the communists, without making any ideological concessions in the process.

THE PHILOSOPHY OF EXISTENCE

The novelty of this lecture lies in the fact that it establishes existentialist philosophy as a clearly defined doctrine. However, this came rather unexpectedly, as Sartre had previously supported the phenomenology of Edmund Husserl (German philosopher and logician, 1859-1938) and Martin Heidegger (German philosopher, 1889-1976).

One of the goals of his short speech was to differentiate his atheistic existentialism from the Christian existentialism represented by thinkers such as Gabriel Marcel (French writer and philosopher, 1889-1973) and Karl Jaspers (German philosopher and psychiatrist, 1883-1969) because existentialism, for the general public, was Sartre. However, Sartre initially rejected the term 'existentialism' which, as he saw it, he had been made to accept after it was forced upon him, and preferred to talk about the philosophy of existence. But no matter what it was called, the thought which Sartre enshrined in doctrine already had its own tradition, with its own influences which its creator made no attempt to conceal.

- With regard to the analysis of existentialist anguish, among other elements, Sartre was greatly inspired by **the work of the Danish philosopher Søren Kierkegaard** (1813-1855), which he also associates with Christian existentialism in *Existentialism and Humanism*.
- Sartrean existentialism has an **important phenomenological basis** (phenomenology being the study of phenomena, of what appears to our conscience. It was first developed by the German philosopher Edmund Husserl at the start of the 20th century). Inspired by Husserl's theory of intentionality, according to which a consciousness must be conscious of something (without which it is nothing), Sartre suggests that the conscious being can be defined as freedom. Moreover, the conscious being is inevitably different from a non-conscious being, in other words all other beings, because it is the only one which needs an object in order to exist (a tree, on the other

hand, is a thing which only needs itself to exist: it is not the tree of something). After all, while it is in the world, the world does not fix consciousness as a thing: it is "in the world" but not "of the world", it is in a constant state of becoming.

- Sartre was also inspired by the **ontology** (the philosophical study of the being as it is) of Martin Heidegger, one of Husserl's followers, whose work *Being and Time* (*Sein und Zeit*, 1927) influenced *Being and Nothingness*. For Heidegger, man is the *Dasein*, the only being which can question its existence. He therefore does not correspond with his being but can relate to it; this fundamental ability defines his existence, which in turn defines the *Dasein*. Sartre uses this definition and, by opposing it to the fixed, definite essence, associates it with freedom.

THE PROBLEM OF POPULARISATION

In order to straighten out any misunderstandings and put right the distorted image the public had of existentialism, Sartre used *Existentialism and Humanism* to try to simplify and popularise it. But, in focusing only on what was essential, he possibly concentrated too much on what the public found problematic to the detriment of everything else. By making his theses more compact and accessible, and by classifying them into a humanist doctrine, it is possible that he impoverished the profound thought present in *Being and Nothingness*.

Moreover, Sartre soon regretted publishing the retranscription of his lecture and, as early as the discussion which immediately followed it, acknowledged that popularisation could weaken his theses. "Sometimes, people who are not capable of fully understanding my theses come to ask me questions. I therefore find myself with two solutions: refuse to answer or accept the discussion while knowing that there will be a degree of popularisation."[1]

He justifies his choice by explaining that weakening a thought to make it understood, like when "theories are introduced in philosophy class"[2], is not necessarily bad, and that, moreover, if existentialism wants to be seen as a philosophy of commitment it must bring out books and become known to the public.

---

1. This quotation has been translated by BrightSummaries.com.
2. This quotation has been translated by BrightSummaries.com.

ANALYSIS

FROM EXISTENTIALISM TO HUMANISM

For Sartre, classic humanism comes down to saying "Man is magnificent!" (p. 54). Using himself as an example of perfection on the basis of certain exceptional feats is absurd ("only the dog or the horse would be in a position to pronounce a general judgment upon man", p. 55): making a cult of a certain idea of humanity only leads to a humanism that is "shut-in upon itself" (*ibid.*).

It is this idea of humanism that Sartre rejects. He rejects this idea of essence and of human nature which can be found in Marxist and Christian humanisms, where man is defined in relation to his sociohistorical practice and in relation to his transcendent aspirations towards the divine respectively. Sartre had recognised in *Being and Nothingness* that man does indeed aspire to a certain fulfilment, to become a perfect being, but that this desire is illusory. Given that man is never perfect, this desire therefore gives him a "useless passion" and makes him suffer because he constantly lacks something. Nevertheless, Sartre himself later rejected this pessimistic perspective.

Having been a prisoner in a stalag (a prisoner camp during the Second World War) in 1940, Sartre experienced human dignity and fraternity. Although he was originally a stubborn individualist, he began to turn towards others and grant importance to intersubjective relations. As the first proof of the new questions he began to ask himself after this defining experience, *Existentialism and Humanism* without a doubt marks a turning point in his intellectual life.

For Sartre, man, who is unable to abandon his freedom and his action, cannot exist without forming himself. It is in this sense that he "is all the time outside of himself" (p. 55) and searches for transcendent goals in order to constantly become himself. However, these goals are always within human understanding, unlike divine transcendence as Christians see it, as something beyond man. This association of the subjectivity of the human universe with a constituent transcendence is existentialist humanism. Existentialism, after the fashion of Heidegger's ontology, confers a unique status upon man. Unlike materialism (which is notably a part of Marxist doctrine), it does not make man one object among many or "a set of pre-determined reactions" (p. 45), but gives him a special kind of dignity. Man is an eternal project, he does not allow himself to be fixed, reduced or determined, he is free: consequently, existentialism is a humanism, because it tries to make man see himself and confront his freedom and what he really is.

THE OPTIMISM OF COMMITMENT

Marxists criticised existentialism for being a quietism and preventing man from acting, by representing him as a being plagued by anguish, incapable of deciding if he is making the right choice or whether it will lead to a result (which seems to signify that all commitment is useless). While it is true that in the end nothing can help man to decide, Sartre counters the Marxists' accusations by underlining that action is necessary even if the choice might appear difficult.

For him, choice is part of human condition, of this part of universality which we all share. We cannot not choose: refusing to choose is still a choice, because this implies our acceptance of the present situation. From the Liberation onwards, Sartre presented himself as a committed intellectual, proclaiming the moral duty of philosophers and writers to take a stand with regard to the events of their time.

TURNING DOWN THE NOBEL PRIZE

On 22 October 1964, Sartre, at the height of his fame, turned down the Nobel Prize in Literature. He was the first person to ever turn down such an honour. Sartre, who got wind of the Swedish Academy's intentions before the official awarding of the prize, decided to write a letter to the Academy secretary on 14 October to make it known that "he [did] not wish to be a Nobel laureate, neither in 1964 nor in the future, and that he will not be able to accept such a distinction"[3] (cited in Pottier, 2015).

However, the decision had already been made, and when the academy confirmed its choice to give the Nobel Prize to the author of *Nausea*, Sartre did not change his position.

He pointed out his "freedom" and remained faithful to

---

3. This quotation has been translated by BrightSummaries.com.

his principles as a committed man: "I deeply regret that this affair has taken on such a scandalous appearance: an award was given out and someone turned it down [...] What I did was not something that I improvised on the spot. I have always turned down official distinctions. [...] The writer must therefore refuse to be transformed into an institution, even if this transformation comes in the most honourable of forms, as is the case here"[4] (cited in Clermont, 2014).

Several years later, he explained the reasons behind his refusal to a journalist: "I turned down the Nobel Prize in Literature because I refused to see myself consecrated before my death. No artist, no writer, no man deserves to be consecrated before his death, because he [still] has the power and freedom to change everything. The Nobel Prize would have raised me up on a pedestal while I had not yet finished accomplishing things, exercising my freedom and acting, committing myself. Every action would have been futile after that, because it would already have been recognised in advance"[5] (cited in Lestienne, 1964).

In *Existentialism and Humanism*, Sartre shows that existentialism does everything it can to make man face the need to act: man is only what he makes of himself, he is nothing more than his actions. He is not defined by what he could have done, by the dreams and ambitions that he did not

---

4. This quotation has been translated by BrightSummaries.com.
5. This quotation has been translated by BrightSummaries.com.

fulfil. An unrealised potential is lost and means nothing. On the other hand, as he is the sum of what he has done, one particular act can never define him entirely: committing one act of cowardice one day, even if it is extreme, still does not make him a coward. Despite the apparent pessimism of existentialism in reality "no doctrine is more optimistic" (p. 44). This optimism prevents man from reducing himself and complaining about what could have been (or, as often happens, using it to console himself in bad faith).

If man, being "condemned to be free" (p. 34), is not formed by his choices and his actions, then they can already be given meaning as the starting point for a system of morality. An existentialist morality is possible as it affirms freedom and judges those who reject it (including those who claim that they cannot exercise it through their choices):

- Since men are alone in the face of absolute freedom, every individual choice involves the whole of humanity ("one ought always to ask oneself what would happen if everyone did as one is doing", pp. 30-31).
- After recognising freedom as the founder of all values, a moral judgement would be that freedom must always be an end in itself and, owing to the fact that that each person has total responsibility (seeing as the freedom of every person involves the freedom of all), every man of good faith cannot help but want the freedom of others.
- There is therefore a certain universality (with freedom as the goal) to the existentialist morality, but it must remain a concrete morality, adapting itself from case to case. Kantian morality, where aiming for freedom also

involves aiming for the freedom of others, restricts itself to considering that an action should be for the good of all and be universally applicable in order to be moral. Since it is purely formal, it falls short in certain concrete situations like the student's dilemma (see "The demand of choice"). Since neither of the two choices (abandoning either his mother if he helps his country or his country if he helps his mother) is universally applicable, neither respects the Kantian moral code. Existentialist morality, on the other hand, dictates that each case must be examined separately: the point is to search for "freedom , in respect of concrete circumstances, can have no other end and aim but itself" (p. 51). It is the job of each person to create their own solution when faced with a concrete moral problem.

The existentialist vision of man gives him absolute, inevitable freedom. He can be pessimistic and go no further than agonising over the uncertainty of his choices, or he can realise that as he is formed by them, they are his only hope. It is in this sense that existentialism becomes "optimistic [...] a doctrine of action" (p. 56).

COHERENT ATHEISM

The starting point of Sartrean existentialism is the non-existence of God; according to Sartre, "Existentialism is nothing else but an attempt to draw the full consequences from a coherent atheistic position" (*ibid.*). This comes from Dostoyevsky's (Russian novelist, 1821-1881) observation that "If God did not exist, everything would be permitted"

(p. 33). The abandonment Sartre spoke of is the absence of God, and above all the consequences of this absence: there are no longer any fixed values of divine right, and man is therefore their only source. The values he chooses are not inscribed anywhere and are never definitive, and nothing forces people to respect them any more. He alone chooses his values because he is no longer justified by God.

Abandonment implies contingency – meaning the free, unnecessary character – of human existence. Anguish, a concept which Sartre borrows from Kierkegaard, is a door leading to the discovery of this contingency, when we feel it, that is. Unlike simple fear, anguish is always about oneself, not about something external: vertigo, for example, is a kind of anguish. We fear not so much the empty space as we do the fact that we could quite easily throw ourselves into it, in spite of every reason we could think of to dissuade ourselves. We realise that the attitude which allows us to stay alive (by not throwing ourselves into the emptiness) is contingent (it can happen or not).

The same thing happens with every choice: anguish is the fear of possibilities, of what we could do, of our liberty (since every possibility is contingent and, in a state of abandonment, permissible) and of our responsibility when faced with choice. Nevertheless, anguish is not an obstacle to action; it is inevitable as it accompanies all awareness of responsibility.

Sartre considers atheistic existentialism, the current that he is a part of, as more coherent than Kierkegaardian and Christian existentialism, since eliminating God brings man back to his contingency: as long as God exists, man cannot truly believe he is free.

FURTHER REFLECTION

- In what way can bad faith bring about a moral judgement? Develop your idea by using examples.
- Explain in what way existentialist morality is a creative morality.
- In your opinion, why does Sartre claim that the cult of humanity "ends in [...] Fascism" (p. 55)?
- In your opinion, how could existentialist relativism turn out to be dangerous?
- Explain how the terms "abandonment", "anguish" and "despair" can have as much of a positive aspect to them as a negative one.
- What do you think about Sartre's ideas about popularisation and commitment?
- Compare Husserl's definition of consciousness with Sartre's vision of man.
- Explain this famous phrase: "existence precedes essence" (p. 28). Camus is also an existentialist thinker. Compare his thought to Sartre's.
- What was the political context of this text when it was published? Explain.

We want to hear from you!
Leave a comment on your online library
and share your favourite books on social media!

FURTHER READING

REFERENCE EDITION

- Sartre, J.P. (1948) *Existentialism and Humanism*. Trans. Mairet, P. London: Meuthen & Co. Ltd.

REFERENCE STUDY

- Flood, A. (2015) Jean-Paul Sartre rejected Nobel prize in a letter to jury that arrived too late. *The Guardian*. [Accessed 9 March 2017]. Available from: <https://www.theguardian.com/books/2015/jan/05/sartre-nobel-prize-literature-letter-swedish-academy>

MORE FROM BRIGHTSUMMARIES.COM

- Reading guide – *No Exit* by Jean-Paul Sartre.
- Reading guide – *Dirty Hands* by Jean-Paul Sartre.

www.brightsummaries.com

Ebook EAN: 9782806294531

Paperback EAN: 9782806294548

Legal Deposit: D/2017/12603/116

This guide was written with the collaboration of Alexandre Randal for the section 'Turning down the Nobel Prize'.

Cover: © Primento

Digital conception by Primento, the digital partner of publishers.